AMERICA'S BLOODIEST SERIAL KILLERS

AMERICA'S BLOODIEST SERIAL KILLERS

From Jeffrey Dahmer
to the Boston Strangler

DR TERRY WESTON

First published in Great Britain by Swordworks Books

ISBN 978-1-906512-49-1

Printed and bound in the UK & US

A catalogue record of this book is available from the British Library

Cover design by Swordworks Books

CONTENTS

INTRODUCTION	7
ALBERT DESALVO	15
TED BUNDY	23
DENNIS LYNN RADER	31
HENRY LEE LUCAS	37
JEFFREY DAHMER	45
DAVID BERKOWITZ	53
WAYNE BERTRAM WILLIAMS	61
PAUL KENNETH BERNARDO	67
JACK KEVORKIAN	73
CONCLUSION	79
OTHER AMERICAN SERIAL KILLERS	85

INTRODUCTION

Serial killers are individuals who have a history of multiple slayings of victims who were generally unknown to them beforehand. Their crimes are committed as a result of a compulsion that, in many but not all cases, has roots in the killer's (often dysfunctional) youth, as opposed to those who are motivated by financial gain (e.g. contract killers) or ideological/political motivations (e.g. terrorists). Many times, this compulsion is linked to the individual's sexual drive.

The term "serial killer" was coined either by FBI agent Robert Ressler or by Dr. Robert Keppel (the credit for the term is still disputed) in the 1970s so that criminologists could distinguish those who claim victims over a long period of time from those who claim multiple victims at once (mass murderers). A third type of multiple killer is a spree killer. The following are brief definitions of these three types:

SERIAL KILLER

A serial killer is someone who commits three or more murders over an extended period of time with cooling-off periods in between. In between their crimes, they appear to be quite normal, a state which Hervey Checkley and Robert Hare call the "mask of sanity." There is frequently—but not always—a sexual element to the murders.

MASS MURDERER

A mass murderer, on the other hand, is an individual who kills three or more people in a single event and in one location. The perpetrators sometimes commit suicide, meaning knowledge of their state of mind and what triggers their actions is often left to more speculation than fact. Mass murderers who are caught sometimes claim they cannot clearly remember the event.

SPREE KILLER

A spree killer commits multiple-murders in different locations over a period of time that may vary from a few hours to several days. Unlike serial killers, however, they do not revert to their normal behaviour in between slayings.

All of the above types of crimes are often carried out

by solitary individuals. There have been examples in all three categories whereby two or more perpetrators have acted together.

Serial killers are generally, but not always, male. Noted female exceptions include Aileen Wuornos and Myra Hindley.

Serial killers are specifically motivated by a variety of psychological urges, primarily power and sexual compulsion. They feel inadequate and worthless, often owing to humiliation and abuse in childhood or the pressures of poverty and low socio-economic status in adulthood, and their crimes give them a feeling of power, both at the time of the actual killing and also afterwards. The knowledge that their actions terrify entire communities and often baffle police forces adds to this sense of power. This motivational aspect separates them from contract killers and other multiple murderers who are motivated by profit. For example, in Scotland during the 1820s, William Burke and William Hare murdered people in what became known as the "Case of the Body Snatchers." They would not count as serial killers by most criminologists' definitions, however, because their motive was financial. Of course, people do things for multiple motivations.

In many cases, a serial killer will plead not guilty by reason of insanity in a court of law. This defense is almost uniformly unsuccessful. The legal definition of insanity is based on whether the defendant knows the difference between right and wrong; the level of premeditation and the lack of any obvious delusions or hallucinations necessary to successfully commit multiple murders without getting caught make this defense extremely difficult.

The United States Bureau of Justice Statistics defines a serial killing as: "involving the killing of several victims in three or more separate events." This definition is especially close to that of a spree killer, and perhaps the primary difference between the two is that a serial killer has a cooling off period. They will commit a murder and, temporarily, feel sated until they feel their homicidal urges resurface. The time period between murders can vary between a few days to several years and will often decrease the longer the offender goes unapprehended. For example, Jeffrey Dahmer murdered his second victim nine years after his first, but his last eight victims were murdered in a space of just seven months. Spree killers, on the other hand, do not have a cooling off period and are in a state of constant hunting until they are caught or killed, even though their murder spree may sometimes extend to a period of several months.

Serial killers frequently have extreme sadistic urges. Ones who lack the ability to empathize with the suffering of others are frequently called psychopathic or sociopathic, terms which have been renamed among professional psychologists as antisocial personality disorder. Some serial killers engage in lust and torture murder, loosely defined terms involving, respectively, mutilation for sexual pleasure and killing victims slowly over a prolonged period of time.

Most serial killers have dysfunctional backgrounds. Frequently they are physically, sexually or psychologically abused as children. There can be a close correlation between their childhood abuse and their crimes. For example, John Wayne Gacy was often beaten by his father and derided as a "sissy" and accused of being homosexual (which he was); in adulthood, Gacy would rape and torture boys and denounce them as being "faggots" and "sissies". Carroll Cole, on the other hand, was abused by his mother, who would engage in extra-marital affairs and force Cole to watch, beating him in order to ensure he did not tell his father. In adulthood, Cole murdered any "loose" woman who reminded him of his mother, in particular married women who were looking for sex behind their husband's back. Some serial killers are seemingly not subjected to any abuse in childhood, although they may have been illegitimate or put up for adoption, or just passed around from relative to relative, creating feelings of being unwanted and rootless. It is often impossible to know exactly what happened in any individual's childhood, so some killers may deny having been abused while others may falsely claim they were abused in an attempt to gain sympathy or tell psychologists what they want to hear.

The element of fantasy in serial killer's development cannot be over-emphasized. They often begin fantasizing about murder during—or even before—adolescence. Their fantasy lives are very rich and they daydream compulsively about dominating and killing people, usually with very specific elements to the murderous fantasy that will eventually be apparent in their real crimes. Some killers are influenced by reading about the Holocaust and fantasize about being in charge of concentration camps. In such cases, however, it is generally not the political ideology of Nazism that they enjoy or are inspired by, but simply an attraction to the brutality and sadism of its application. Others enjoy reading the works of Marquis de Sade, who lends his name to the word "sadism" due to his stories, which were packed with rape, torture and murder. Many use pornography, frequently the violent type involving bondage, although they may also read "detective magazines" that feature stories of real life homicide cases. Others may even be fascinated and aroused by less obviously disagreeable material. Dahmer, for example, was fascinated by the character of Emperor Palpatine in Return of the Jedi, and even bought yellow contact lenses to make himself resemble the evil character, while several killers say their fantasies have been influenced by The Bible, in particular the Book of Revelation.

Some serial killers display one or more of what are known as the "MacDonald Triad" of warning signs in childhood. These are:

- Firestarting, invariably just for the thrill of destroying things.
- Cruelty to Animals. Most children can be cruel to animals, such as pulling the legs off of spiders, but future serial killers often kill larger animals, like dogs and cats, and frequently for their solitary enjoyment rather than to impress peers.
- Bedwetting beyond the age when children normally grow out of such behaviour.

Most serial killers claim their first victim when they are in their twenties, although this can vary, with one killer claiming the first of his victims when he was 38, and another who was just 15 when he admitted to murdering four people during the previous two years. On average, serial killers start murdering people when they are in their early-to-mid-twenties.

It has been claimed by many experts that once serial killers start that they cannot (or only rarely) stop. Recently this view has been called into question as new serial killers are caught through methods that were previously unavailable, like DNA testing. Some argue that those who are unable to control their homicidal impulses are more easily caught and thus overrepresented in the statistics.

The rate at which they claim victims can also vary a great deal, and even though the US produces more serial killers than any other country in the world, the concept is not an inherently American and Great Britain is not immune to the horrific realities of serial killers.

ALBERT DESALVO

Born

September 3, 1931

Also known as:
The Boston Strangler

Number of victims:
13

THE BOSTON STRANGLER

There was no sign of forced entry. They knew him or they let him in. Thirteen women, all single, died in Boston between June 14, 1962 and January 4, 1964. They were sexually molested and strangled with articles of clothing in their apartments. The police were never sure one assailant was responsible even though Albert DeSalvo confessed to eleven of the killings. The public, however, was convinced – perhaps because it was more comforting to believe that a killer was behind bars. But many questions remain unanswered to this day, including whether DeSalvo was guilty at all.

The Strangler Case was not DeSalvo's first brush with the law. Between 1956 and 1960 he was arrested multiple times for breaking and entering, receiving a suspended sentence each time. In 1961, however, DeSalvo was arrested for gaining entrance into women's homes on the pretext of measuring them for a fictitious modeling agency. He was sentenced to 18 months but was released early for good behavior, just two months before the Strangler claimed his first victim.

In October 27, 1964 DeSalvo posed as a police detective to gain entrance to a young woman's home. He tied her to the bed, fondled her, apologized, and left. The woman's description of her assailant reminded detectives of the "Measuring Man." When they picked up DeSalvo the woman conclusively identified him. He was set free on bail, but when his photo was released, numerous women called in identifying him as an area rapist known as the Green Man because he always wore green work plants. With the braggadocio that was his nature, DeSalvo claimed to have assaulted as many as 300 women in a four-state area.

DeSalvo was sent to the Bridgewater State Hospital for observation. There he became friends with George Nassar, a violent man charged with the execution-style killing of a gas station attendant. With a near genius-level IQ, Nassar was a skilled manipulator who had already been to prison for murder. He spent his time behind bars studying Russian.

DeSalvo was not even a suspect in the Strangler case so why did he suddenly confess to the killings? The answer may lie with George Nassar. Apparently while at Bridgwater DeSalvo became worried about how his family would survive monetarily when he went to jail. There was a reward of $10,000 for information leading to the arrest and conviction of the Strangler. DeSalvo and Nassar discussed it, mistakenly assuming the amount was $10,000 per victim. If Nassar turned him in and DeSalvo confessed they agreed to split the money. Nassar's attorney was F. Lee Bailey, famous for his handling of the Dr. Sam Sheppard case. Bailey took a Dictaphone to Bridgewater and recorded DeSalvo's confession.

DeSalvo's confession was lengthy and detailed, filling 50 hours of tapes and running to 2,000 typed pages. There was, however, one nagging problem. No shred of physical evidence was ever uncovered to corroborate his confession. Consequently, DeSalvo only stood trial for the robberies and sexual offenses unrelated to the Strangler case. Still, he was sentenced to life in prison in 1967 where he was murdered six years later – some say because he was set to reveal the real identity of the Strangler.

There were many inconsistencies in the Strangler case, including those raised by a number of eyewitnesses.

- An engineering student who lived above one of the victims spoke to a stranger looking for directions the night of the murder. The student didn't recognize DeSalvo.

- A woman who saw a man standing in a victim's bathroom window didn't recognize DeSalvo.
- A third witness worked with a police sketch artist to develop an image of the man who came to her door claiming to be a painter and then left when she said her husband was home. She described a light-skinned man with straight, blond hair combed back from an oval face. The sketch bore absolutely no resemblance to DeSalvo. The woman did, however, believe George Nassar was the man she saw. Everything fit but his hair color.
- And a fourth woman, who actually fought off the Strangler didn't recognize DeSalvo but became violently agitated when she saw Nassar.

Reputedly DeSalvo possessed a photographic memory. Critics of the case argued that he was coached by Nassar. Even if Nassar wasn't the killer, experts were never convinced the Strangler killings were the work of a single man. The victims ranged in age from 19 to 85 and did not represent one body type, race, or lifestyle. There was no set pattern in the killings with one victim being discreetly tucked in bed while another was brutally violated with a broom handle.

In October 2001 DeSalvo's body and that of one of his victims were both exhumed in order to perform DNA testing. In December it was announced that the samples taken from the remains of Strangler victim Mary Sullivan did not match DeSalvo. While James E. Starrs, professor of forensic sciences at George Washington University pointed out that the findings only cleared DeSalvo of sexual assault, he also said, "If I was a juror, I would acquit him with no questions asked." Sullivan's family insists that police had a viable candidate for the Strangler murders before DeSalvo's confession and claims – chillingly – that the suspect is still alive and well in New England today.

TED BUNDY

Born

November 24, 1946

Also known as:
Chris Hagen
Richard Burton
Officer Roseland
Rolf Miller

Number of victims:
26-35+

FLA DOC
D
A069 063
FEB 13 1980

TED BUNDY

Theodore Robert Bundy didn't look like a murderer, but he killed at least 36 women. This charming, handsome, well-educated man bludgeoned and raped his victims and then mutilated and molested their corpses.

Experts argue about whether Bundy was a sociopath or a psychopath. Either way, he was one of America's most notorious and well-documented serial killers. We may never really know what triggered his bloody career. Raised to believe his grandparents were in fact his parents, he did not discover until sometime in 1969 that his "sister" was actually his birth mother.

From an awkward and shy pre-adolescent, Ted blossomed into a well-dressed, well-mannered high school student. He didn't date, but spent his time skiing and nursing a fascination for politics. In college he worked on a Washington gubernatorial re-election campaign making many Republican party contacts.

While in college, Bundy became infatuated with a wealthy California girl. When she dumped him, Ted was devastated. He obsessed about her for years until he reconnected with her. Bundy made her fall in love with him again only to reject her as thoroughly as she had spurned him. It was a long-planned revenge and one that offers insight into the workings of Bundy's mind.

At roughly the same time Bundy learned the truth about his family he began to steal – first small items from work or school, then shoplifting and finally burglary. At the same time, however, he re-enrolled at the University of Washington, studied psychology, and became a well-liked honors student.

Bundy's first confirmed assault occurred at the University on January 4, 1974. After midnight he slipped into the basement bedroom of 18-year-old Joni Lenz and beat her mercilessly with a crowbar. He then sexually assaulted her with a steel rod from her bed frame. Amazingly, Lenz survived. She was discovered comatose in a pool of blood the next morning and suffered permanent brain damage.

On January 31, Bundy entered the bedroom of 21-year-old senior Lynda Ann Healy. He knocked her unconscious, dressed her in jeans and a shirt, and carried Healy away wrapped in a bed sheet. A year later authorities discovered the decapitated remains in the mountains east of Seattle.

Between January and June 1974 Bundy stalked and killed at least eight women. All were single, white, and slender with long hair parted in the middle. They all disappeared in the evening and all wore slacks. Some witnesses in the area of the disappearances reported seeing a man wearing a cast, struggling with books, and asking young women for help. Sometimes the man said he was having trouble starting his Volkswagen "bug."

In August 1974 in Lake Sammamish State Park authorities identified a few strands of hair, five thigh bones, two skulls, and a jaw bone as all that remained of Janice Ott and Denise Naslund. The last people who saw Ott alive said she was approached by a handsome man named Ted who asked for help to load his boat. His arm was in a cast. Naslund walked to a park restroom and was never seen again. That same afternoon a man in an arm cast was asking women to help him load a boat.

Suddenly that fall, the disappearances stopped. No one knew it was because Ted Bundy had moved to Salt Lake City to attend law school. There, he raped, sodomized, and strangled 17-year-old Melissa Smith and did the same thing to Laura Aime twelve days later on Halloween.

On November 8, 1974 Bundy made a critical mistake. He allowed Carol DaRonch to escape. Posing as a police officer, Bundy lured her into his VW where he attempted to handcuff her. DaRonch wrenched the door open and

Bundy came after her with a crowbar. DaRonch kicked him in the genitals and ran.

In the end, that tan VW bug was Bundy's undoing. It was seen in the parking lot of Viewmont High School when Debby Kent disappeared. At the same site, authorities also found a small key that fit the handcuffs Carol DaRonch had worn.

With things getting hot for him in Utah, Bundy went on the road, killing Caryn Campbell in Colorado in January 1975. The cause of death was blunt force head trauma. Before he was done, five women in the state died in the same way.

On August 16, 1975 a tan VW bug sped away from police in Salt Lake County. When the driver finally did stop, police found the car's passenger seat missing. Inside was a crowbar, ski mask, rope, handcuffs, wire, and an ice pick. Bundy was immediately arrested.

The connections to DaRonch and Kent fell into place quickly. The more authorities learned about Ted Bundy the more convinced they became that they had their man. His girlfriend even told investigators he had plaster of Paris in his room for making casts.

Bundy was sentenced to fifteen years in Utah for kidnapping DaRonch. He was then taken to Colorado to stand trial for murder. During a recess, however, Bundy escaped through a second-story window. He was recaptured a week later. Back in jail he escaped again cutting a hole in the ceiling of his cell and simply walking out the front door. He stole a car and drove away.

Reaching Florida in January 1978, Bundy bludgeoned two sleeping women and wounded two others in a Chi Omega sorority house in Tallahassee. His last victim was 12-year-old Kimberly Leach in Lake City. On the 15th he was apprehended in Pensacola – driving a stolen, orange VW bug.

In 1979 when Bundy was convicted of murder after defending himself, Judge Edward Coward sentenced him to death saying, "It's a tragedy for this court to see such a total waste of humanity as I've experienced in this courtroom . . . you went the wrong way, partner."

Bundy died in the Florida electric chair at age 42 on January 24, 1989. Guards say he had to be dragged from his cell.

DENNIS LYNN RADER

Born

March 9, 1945

Also known as:
Ethan Truman
Bill Thomas Killman
BTK
The BTK Murderer
The BTK Killer
The BTK Strangler

Number of victims:
10

THE BTK MURDERER

He described his victims as “projects” and said of his victims that he “put them down.” Dennis Lynn Rader, the BTK killer, confessed to everything in a Wichita, Kansas courtroom on June 27, 2005. He was calm, detached, almost clinical as he discussed his misdeeds between 1974 and 1991. Rader received ten consecutive life sentences – one for reach of his victims.

Except for a four-year stint in the Air Force, Rader spent his entire life in Wichita, attending high school and college there and holding down various jobs including supervisor for the Compliance Department of the suburb of Park City from 1991 to 2005. He was also president of the Congregation Council of Christ Lutheran Church where he had been a member for 30 years and he was Cub Scout leader. In 1971 he married Paula Dietz and both of their children were born after the BTK murders began. (Paula was granted an immediate divorce in Sedgwick County court on July 27, 2005.)

Rader used a briefcase or bowling bag to assemble his "hit kit," which contained a gun, tape, rope, and handcuffs as well as "hit clothes" to be worn during the crime and then disposed of. He wandered the city looking for his next "project," picking out an individual and then stalking them to learn the pattern of their lives and to pick the best time to "put them down." An efficient man, Rader often had several projects under development, always having a back-up plan in the event a victim didn't work out. When he was ready to strike, Rader broke into the victim's house, cut the phone lines, and waited for his prey to come home. He calmed his victims by posing as a rapist, claiming he simply needed to work out his sexual fantasies.

Rader himself chose the name "BTK" for its precise description of his methods. First he strangled a victim to unconsciousness, then revived them and did it again – over and over and over. He was sexually aroused by the sight of their repeated near-death experiences. Finally, when he was ready, Rader strangled them to death before masturbating and ejaculating onto the corpse.

Not content to taunt his victims, Rader also taunted local police and newspapers with a series of letters between 1974 and 1979. He stashed the first in an engineering book in the Wichita Public Library in October, 1974 that described in detail his killings of four members of the Otero family the previous January. In his letter to television station KAKE in early 1978, Rader claimed responsibility for the Oteros, Shirley Vian, Nancy Fox, and another victim most probably Kathryn Bright. It was in this communique that he suggested the name BTK for himself, demanding media attention.

In a particularly chilling act of intimidation, Rader sent two identical packages in 1979, one to an intended victim who was not home when he broke into her home and another to KAKE. The package included a poem entitled, "Oh Anna Why Didn't You Appear" and a drawing of what he had intended to to do to Anna Williams had she come home. He waited inside her home for several hours and to prove it, he sent along a few small items he'd picked up while there. In all his letters Rader wrote poorly with misspelling and incorrect grammar. Authorities assumed it was a ruse to hide the killer's intelligence but Rader, although he earned a college degree in 1979, is really that poor a writer. In 1988 when three members of the Fager family were killed in Wichita, Rader sent authorities a note just to let them know the crime wasn't one of his, although he felt the murderer had done admirable work.

Beginning in March 2004 Rader began a series of eleven communications which culminated in his arrest in February 2005. Using the pseudonymn Bill Thomas

Killman on the return address of a letter to The Wichita Eagle, Rader enclosed a photocopy of Vicki Wegerle's driver's license and took credit for her September 1986 murder. He sent word puzzles, he taped packages to stop signs, he left material in the drop box at the public library – Rader even threatened the life of lead investigator Lt. Ken Landwehr. He was behaving like a man who wanted to be caught and his final mistake was almost ridiculously naive. In a communication to police he asked if a computer disk was traceable. Of course they said no. On February 16, 2005 Rader put his writings on a disk and sent it to television station KSAS. Forensic analysis found data embedded in a Microsoft Word document that pointed to Christ Lutheran Church. The document was last modified by "Dennis." Police simple did a Google search and found out Dennis Rader was the church president.

After obtaining medical records for Rader's daughter Kerri, a DNA test confirmed a familial relationship to semen collected at a BTK crime scene. Rader was taken into custody on February 25, 2005 and his home, car, and church office were searched. Rader confessed immediately, talking for hours and filling up twelve DVDs with his confession. Among other things, he said he'd resumed taunting the police because now, with his children grown, he was bored.

HENRY LEE LUCAS

Born

August 23, 1936

Also known as:
The Confession Killer

Number of victims:
3-3000

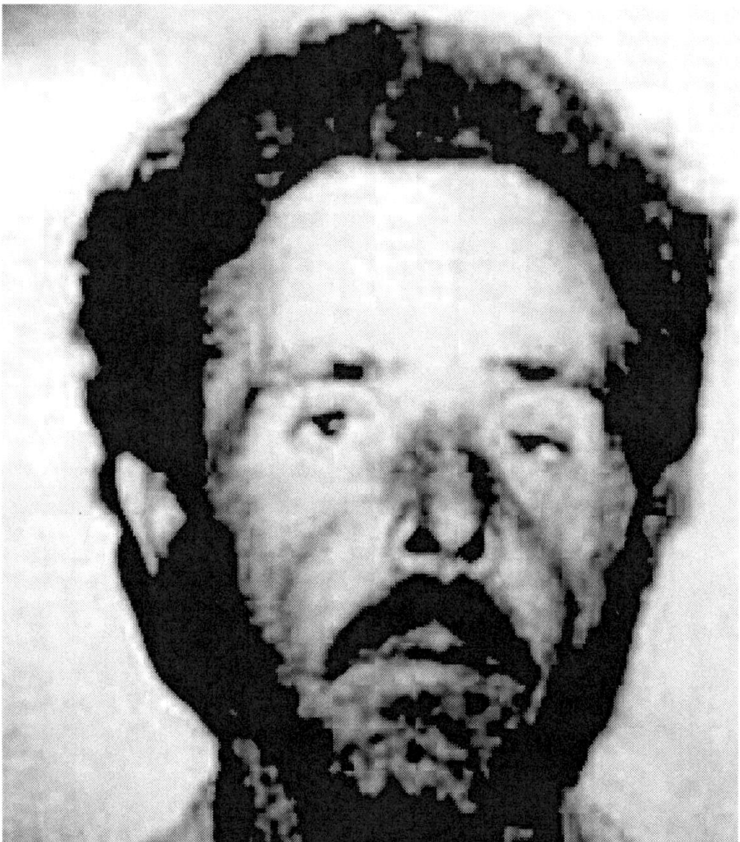

THE CONFESSION KILLER

If Ted Bundy was handsome, urbane, and polished, Henry Lee Lucas was anything but. One thing Bundy and Lucas did have in common, however, was that they liked to talk. Altogether Lucas may have confessed to as many 3,000 murders, authorities deemed only 350 to be plausible and Lucas later recanted many of his confessions. Consequently, determining the true extent of his crime spree, sometimes in the company of his lover and accomplice, Ottis Toole, is difficult at best.

Lucas claimed to have first killed in 1951 but his first confirmed murder was that of his mother in January 1960 in Tecumseh, Michigan. The two argued over Lucas' plans to marry. He claimed Viola Lucas returned home drunk and began beating him with a broom while he slept. He said he stabbed her in the neck in self defense. Lucas was convicted of second-degree murder with a sentence of 20 to 40 years of which he served 15 before being released in August 1975. Later in his career when psychologists sought to evaluate Lucas, they determined his violent misogyny stemmed from his deep-seated hatred of his mother.

After serving a second, three-year stint for attempted kidnapping, Lucas was briefly married. When his wife accused him of molesting her daughters, Lucas hit the road, roaming throughout the American South and working at odd jobs. Between 1976 and 1978 he met Ottis Toole. It was an odd relationship that also involved Toole's niece Frieda Powell whom the men called "Becky." In 1982 Lucas and Becky moved to Texas, an act of betrayal in Toole's eyes that reputedly led him to kill nine people in six state over the next thirteen months.

After living briefly with 82-year-old Kate Rich in Ringgold, Texas, Lucas and Powell settled at a religious commune in Stoneburg, "The House of Prayer." When Becky disappeared, Lucas claimed the two had quarreled at a truck stop in Bowie, where Powell hitched a ride with a trucker back to Florida. Authorities did not believe him and grew more suspicious of his activities when Rich also disappeared. She was seen with Lucas the day she went missing.

It was later revealed that Lucas stabbed Becky after she slapped him. He raped the corpse next to an interstate highway then removed the head and cut the body into nine pieces. He scattered the parts around a nearby field. Three weeks later he killed Kate Rich and molested her corpse. A month later he retrieved the remains and incinerated them in a stove at the House of Prayer. Lucas later directed authorities to the remains and effects of both women.

Already under suspicion for two murders, Lucas was actually arrested for possession of a firearm in June 1983, a violation of his parole. While in custody, Lucas confessed to both the murders. Later he attributed his enthusiastic confessions to mistreatment at the hands of police. Lucas claimed he was held naked in a small cell without bedding for four days with no opportunity to speak to a lawyer. The accuracy with which he led authorities to what remained of both women and their personal effects did confirm he had killed them even if his subsequent confessions were later called into doubt.

In a Montague County courtroom Lucas said, “I killed Kate Rich and at least a hundred more.” In the wake of his startling assertion, the Texas Department of Public Safety contacted jurisdictions around the state to arrange interviews with Lucas to clear unsolved cases from the books. For his part, Lucas enjoyed his new found fame enormously, talking happily with authorities and looking forward to field trips.

Certainly Lucas knew details and could often lead police to physical remains, but it is possible that his friend and traveling companion Ottis Toole was the real killer. Toole's IQ put him just above mental retardation. He was both an arsonist and a serial killer, raised by a mother who was a religious fanatic and a grandmother with an interest in Satanism. Toole killed a traveling salesman when he was 14 and was a suspect in four other murders before he met Lucas.

When the men began traveling together they preyed on hitchhikers – females for Lucas and males for Toole. They also committed robberies, killing their victims to silence them as witnesses. Toole, already in prison for other crimes, readily confirmed everything Lucas said and added his own details. Thanks to his contributions it seemed that another two dozen murders in eleven states were cleared.

In 1983 at a one-day event sponsored by the DPS Lucas was questioned by lawmen from all over Texas. He took credit for 126 murders, 35 of which officers believed to be clearly connected to him. In January 1984 out-of-state officers had their chance and believed they cleared 72 cases perpetrated by Lucas and Toole and identified 71 others in which they may have been involved.

Tried in San Angelo, Texas in March 1984 for the 1979 death of a woman near Georgetown, Lucas was found guilty and sentenced to death. And then he started talking to various reporters, dramatically changing his story, saying the only person he ever killed was his mother. By June 1984 many cases that had been cleared by Lucas' confessions were quietly reopened.

In 1996, Ottis Toole died in a Florida prison of cirrhosis of the liver. He was serving multiple life sentences. In the only commutation he ever handed down, then-Texas Governor George W. Bush commuted Lucas' sentence to life. In prison Lucas grew fat and complacent, dying of natural causes in March 2001, still playing his games with law enforcement. He clearly committed at least four murders. He was convicted of eleven. He may have been responsible for forty or fifty others. While the numbers will never be conclusively sorted out, one thing is for sure, Lucas thoroughly enjoyed his life of crime, often at the expense of the authorities.

JEFFREY DAHMER

Born
May 21, 1960

Number of victims:
17 killed

JEFFREY DAHMER

On November 28, 1994 a fellow inmate beat Jeffrey Dahmer and double murder Christopher Scarver to death with a bench-press bar in the weight room of the Colombia Correctional Institute in Portage, Wisconsin. Convicted on fifteen counts of murder and sentenced to 936 years, most people regarded death as too easy for the serial killer, cannibal, and necrophiliac.

Dahmer, a closet homosexual and alcoholic, was intensely shy from early childhood and suffered from a severe lack of self-esteem. He committed his first murder at 18 when he invited hitchhiker Steven Hicks to his home. They had sex and drank beer together. Dahmer "didn't want him to leave," striking the man in the head with a barbell, dismembering the body, and burying the parts in garbage bags behind his parents home in Bath, Ohio.

After flunking out of Ohio State University, Dahmer joined the army in 1978 and served as a medic in Germany but was discharged for alcoholism. One of the first things he did when he returned home was to dig up Hick's body, pound the remains with a sledgehammer, and scatter them in the woods.

In 1981 Dahmer was arrested for drunken and disorderly conduct and again in 1986 for masturbating in front of two boys. For the latter offense, Dahmer received a year's probation. A year later, in September 1987, he killed his second victim, Steven Toumi, in a hotel room. He then took the corpse to his grandmother's basement and performed sexual acts with the body before dismembering it and throwing it in the garbage.

A few months later, by the time Dahmer selected his third victim, fourteen-year-old Jamie Doxtator, the killer had developed his routine. Normally he met his victims at gay bars or bathhouses where he would offer them money to pose for photographs or invite them home for beer and a video. Dahmer would then drug the men, strangle them, have sex with or masturbate on the corpse, dismember it, and dispose of the remains keeping the skull or other parts as souvenirs.

Although Dahmer's grandmother had no idea what Jeff was doing in her basement, she did tire of the noise and drunkenness and insisted he leave. He moved into a Milawukee apartment and the next day offered a

13-year-old boy $50 to pose for photos, then drugged and fondled him. After the boy's parents took him to the hospital, police arrested Dahmer for sexual exploitation and assault. He pleaded guilty and while he waited to be sentenced, Dahmer moved back to his grandmother's where he killed 24-year-old Anthony Sears.

Although three psychologists who examined Dahmer at the time reported that he needed intense psychological treatment in a resident facility, Dahmer gave an eloquent and persuasive performance before the judge, blaming his behavior on alcoholism, professing a great affection for his job at a chocolate factory, and exhibiting an obviously sincere desire to turn his life around. The judge bought it all and Dahmer was sentenced to five years' probation, a year in a work release unit, and was required to register as a sex offender.

When Dahmer was released after ten months for good behavior he moved to Apartment 213 at 924 North 25th Street and began killing in earnest. In the next fifteen months, he murdered twelve men. In one of the most outrageous episodes of his sordid career, on the night of May 26, 1991 Dahmer convinced police that 14-year-old Konerak Sinthasomphone was his 19-year-old gay lover and simply intoxicated. At the time Sinthasomphone was naked, dazed, and bleeding from the head. Police even accompanied Dahmer and Sinthasomphone back to Dahmer's apartment where they did note a bad smell. (It was the body of Tony Hughes that had been decomposing in the bedroom for three days.) Dahmer apologized for the disturbance and promised it wouldn't happen again. Believing his story and judging they had better things to do then arbitrate a spate between gay lovers, the police left. Later that night Dahmer dismembered Sinthasomphone and kept his skull for a souvenir.

By the summer of 1991 Dahmer was murdering one victim per week. On the night of July 22, however, Tracy Edwards escaped Dahmer's apartment and flagged down a squad car. With one handcuff still dangling from his wrist, Edwards led police to Dahmer. What they found was one of the most horrific killing dens in the annals of American crime.

The apartment contained the remains of eleven victims. Officers found skulls in the refrigerator and photographs in the bedroom depicting men before, during, and after their suffering at Dahmer's hands. In the back of the bedroom closet they found a metal stockpot that contained decomposed hands and a penis. Two skulls sat on a shelf above the vat. The same closet contained ethyl alcohol, chloroform and jars of formaldehyde with preserved male genitalia.

When Dahmer admitted eating the biceps of his eighth victim, Ernest Miller, whose skeleton he also kept, Dahmer casually said human flesh "tasted like meat" to him. He did express the belief that by consuming his victims their life essence would be transferred to him and said the cannibalism gave him an erection. Because control was critical to Dahmer, he also attempted crude lobotomies, drilling holes in the mens' skulls after they were drugged and injecting them with muriatic acid. He claimed all died but one who functioned at a minimal level for a few days before expiring. Additionally, Dahmer dabbled in Satanism and said his deeds made him feel "thoroughly evil."

Anyone reading Dahmer's 160-page confession would agree. He pleaded guilty by reason of insanity making his trial a macabre parade of details, descriptions, and images that both fascinated and disgusted the jury and the world. After five hours of deliberations Dahmer was found guilty and sane. Although initially isolated from the prison populace, Dahmer was a model prisoner who talked authorities into letting him have more contact with the general population. This time, however, Dahmer's persuasiveness cost him his own life.

DAVID BERKOWITZ

Born
June 1, 1953

Also known as:
The Son of Sam
.44 Callibre Killer

Number of victims:
6 killed, 7 wounded

THE SON OF SAM

The papers originally called him the ".44 Caliber Killer," referring to the killer's favored weapon to hunt, maim, and murder women throughout New York City. At the scene of one of his crimes on April 17, 1977, however, a rambling letter set authorities straight on his identify. "I am deeply hurt by your calling me a [woman] . . . hater," it read.

"I am not. But I am a monster. I am the 'Son of Sam.'

A week earlier a Yonkers resident, Sam Carr received a letter complaining about his black Labrador, Harvey, followed by a death threat on April 19. Then, on April 29, a man in jeans and a yellow shirt shot the dog. Harvey lived and police began an investigation, but because the "Son of Sam" letter had not yet been leaked, no connection was made between the two incidents.

The killer's first attack occurred on the morning of July 29, 1976. Donna Lauria, 18, and Jody Valenty, 19, sat talking in Jody's car outside Donna's apartment building around 1 a.m. Suddenly Donna noticed a man standing on the passenger side. Without warning he took out a large handgun, squatted, and fired five times into the car. Donna died instantly of a neck wound, Jody, hit in the thigh, leaned on the horn.

Three months later, on October 23, Carl Cenaro give Rosemary Keenan a ride home from a Queen's bar. They were talking in the parked car when a man appeared on the passenger side, drew a gun, and fired five times striking Carl in the head. The terrified Rosemary drove the car back to the bar where friends rushed Carl to the hospital. Surgeons replaced part of his skull with a metal plate.

A month later on November 26, Donna DeMasi, 16, and Joanne Lomino, 18, got off a bus near Joanne's home. A man followed them and made as if to ask for directions. Instead, he pulled a gun from beneath his jacket and emptied it into the girls. Donna survived and Joanne was left a paraplegic.

Two months passed before the next attack on January 30, 1977. Christine Freund, 26, and her fiance John Dahl had just gotten into his car around 12:10 a.m. when two shots shattered the windshield. Both bullets struck Christine in the head. She died a few hours later in the hospital.

On March 8, 1977 Virginia Voskerichian, Barnard College honor student, was walking home from classes when a man approached her, pulled out a gun, and fired. A single shot struck her in the face killing her instantly. As the assailant ran away he passed a witness and said, "Hi, mister." The bullet recovered from Voskerichian matched the one that killed Donna Lauria, confirming for the police that they were looking for a single shooter. Ultimately more than 200 detectives worked on the Operation Omega task to apprehend the Son of Sam.

On April 17, Valentina Suriana, 18, and Alexander Esau, 21, were necking in a parked car near the Hutchinson River Parkway. At 3 a.m. a car pulled up beside their vehicle and shot them both. Valentina died on the scene, Alexander later at the hospital. But this time, the killer did something different, he left his "Son of Sam" letter at the scene.

As the police tracked down leads from checking registrations on .44 caliber handguns to tracing the activities of released mental patients, the Son of Sam sent a letter to Daily News reporter Jimmy Breslin. "Sam's a thirsty lad," it said, "He won't let me stop killing until he gets his fill of blood." Partial fingerprints were lifted from the letter.

David Berkowitz came to the attention of police when New Rochelle resident Jack Cassara received a note ostensibly from Sam Carr including a photo of a German shepherd. Meeting with Carr, Cassara learned of Harvey's shooting and that of a neighborhood German shepherd. Later Cassara's son remembered a strange man. David Berkowitz, who briefly rented a room from them in early 1976. Berkowitz was always bothered by the family dog.

At 3 a.m. on June 26 Judy Placido had just said to Sal Lupo, "This Son of Sam is really scary," when a blast echoed in the car. Horrified, Sal ran into the disco for help and Judy looked in the mirror. She was covered in blood; she had been hit three times, Sal was wounded once.

The Son of Sam took his last victims on July 31, 1977. Stacy Moskowitz and Bobby Violante were sitting in his father's car near Gravesend Bay in Brooklyn. Bobby was shot twice in the face and Stacy once in the head. Thirty-eight hours later Stacy died in the hospital. Bobby lost his left eye and had only 20% vision remaining in his right.

When it was discovered that a traffic ticket was issued to David Berkowitz in the vicinity that night, all the pieces began to fall into place. On August 10 when police surrounded Berkowitz in his car, he smiled at them. Ordered to identify himself he said, "I'm Sam. David Berkowitz."

Experiencing anger and frustration with women while engaging in a bizarre fantasy life, Berkowitz recorded more than 1,488 acts of arson in his diary before demons began tormenting him with orders to kill. He gave in to the voices hoping to silence them with his compliance.

In 1975 he stabbed two women, temporarily pacifying the demons. When Berkowitz moved to the Cassara's he became convinced that howling dogs formed a devil's army roaming the streets craving blood. The black Lab Harvey pushed Berkowitz over the edge. Berkowitz saw the dog as Sam Carr's servant and believed Carr to be a powerfully evil demon.

Berkowitz pleaded guilty and received 365 years in jail. At a parole hearing in 2002 Berkowitz, a jail house convert to Christianity, said frankly he does not deserve to be released. Claiming to struggle with the things he has done, he believes he is where he belongs. The parole board agreed.

WAYNE BERTRAM WILLIAMS

Born
May 27, 1958

Also Known As
The Atlanta Monster
The Atlanta Child Killer
The Atlanta Child Murderer

Number of victims:
2-31 killed

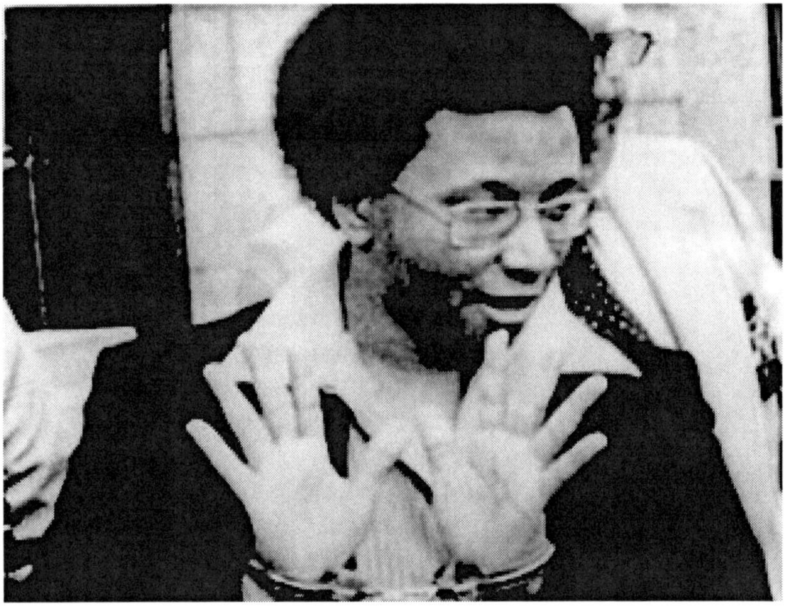

THE ATLANTA MONSTER

Between 1979 and 1981 twenty-nine African-American children were murdered in Atlanta, Georgia. The boys were asphyxiated and their nude bodies dumped in area rivers. After an unusual incident on a bridge, the key suspect in the case became Wayne Williams. He was not, however convicted of killing the children but rather of murdering two adult men. Williams' tie to the child murders remains controversial twenty-five years later. At the time, one incident in particular proved particularly damning against him.

Many of the bodies were found near the James Jackson Parkway Bridge over the Chattahoochee River. On May 22, 1981 two police officers on stake-out at the bridge heard a loud splash. Officer Freddie Jacobs said he saw a car's headlights crossing the bridge and almost immediately received a radio call from Officer Bob

Campbell who was positioned beneath the structure. Campbell heard a splash and looking up, saw a car on the bridge. As Jacobs watched, the car, a white 1970 Chevrolet station wagon, crossed the bridge, turned around, and came back again. A third police officer, Carl Holden, was parked at a liquor store on the far side of the bridge. He followed the car. When FBI agents pulled the car over half a mile away it was being driven by 23-year-old Wayne Williams.

Williams, a music promoter and freelance photographer gave police a fictitious name and address for a client he claimed to have been meeting that night. Hours later authorities dragged the river but found no body. The next day, however, when they questioned Williams further they realized he was, at best, an odd duck. Williams owned his own own radio station, and in spite of rather a tin ear, promoted local musical talent. He fiddled with electronics as a hobby and sold video footage and photographs of accidents. Consequently, he routinely listened to the police scanner and often arrived on the scene of an incident before the cops. Williams had a reputation for lying and bragging. He lived with his parents and had few friends – and he was known to impersonate a police officer and had outfitted his car with illegal red flashing lights beneath the grille and a blue strobe for the dashboard.

When the nude body of Nathaniel Cater was pulled from

the Chattahoochee on May 24, 1981 the medical examiner obligingly made the time of death fit the incident on the bridge. Even though four witnesses later came forward saying they had seen Cater alive after May 22, Williams became the prime suspect not just in his death but also in the child murders. In the end, however, Williams was tried only for the murder of two adults, Cater and Jimmy Payne. Georgia law allowed the prosecution to bring in evidence from other cases in order to establish a "pattern," which is how trace evidence from the child killings was used against Williams.

Prosecutors matched nineteen fiber sources from Williams' home to a number of murder victims including fibers from his bedspread, carpets, clothes – and even his dog. Eyewitnesses claimed to have seem him with different victims and the blood of various victims was found in his car. Additionally, it was rumored that Williams was a homosexual interested in young boys. And then there was the incident on the bridge. After two months of testimony, the jury took just ten hours to sentence Williams to two consecutive life sentences. But still, questions remain.

The evidence associated with the two cars owned by the Williams family is some of the most troublesome. Williams did not have access to the vehicles during three of the six murders linked to the cars by fiber evidence. A 1979 Ford was in the shop for repairs five hours before one victim disappeared and was not returned to the family until after the boy was already dead. The car was put in the shop again the next morning when it was still not functioning properly and was left there because the new repair estimate was too high. Another victim died twelve days before the Williams' family purchased the second car, a 1970 Chevrolet, which authorities claimed contained trace evidence from the boy in question.

The case was highly charged emotionally and racially and it has been argued that once Williams was in custody, witnesses came forward with startling convenience. It is also interesting that in 1985 evidence was uncovered linking the Ku Klux Klan, an infamous hate group, to the child killings as well as to a string of unsolved murders of black women from 1980 to 1982. The groups' apparent desire in committing the crimes was to spark a race war.

Williams' appeals for a new trial based on inconsistencies and suppressed evidence were denied, however. With the passage of time though, authorities have become less convinced of his guilt. In 2005, four of the cases attributed to Williams were reopened by DeKalb County Police Chief Louis Graham who believes Williams may be innocent of all of the murders. Williams, for his part, has continued to vehemently deny any involvement in the killings – denials all emanating from his jail cell.

PAUL KENNETH BERNARDO

Born
August 27, 1964

Also Known As
Paul Teale
The Scarborough Rapist
The Schoolgirl Killer

Number of victims:
3+ killed

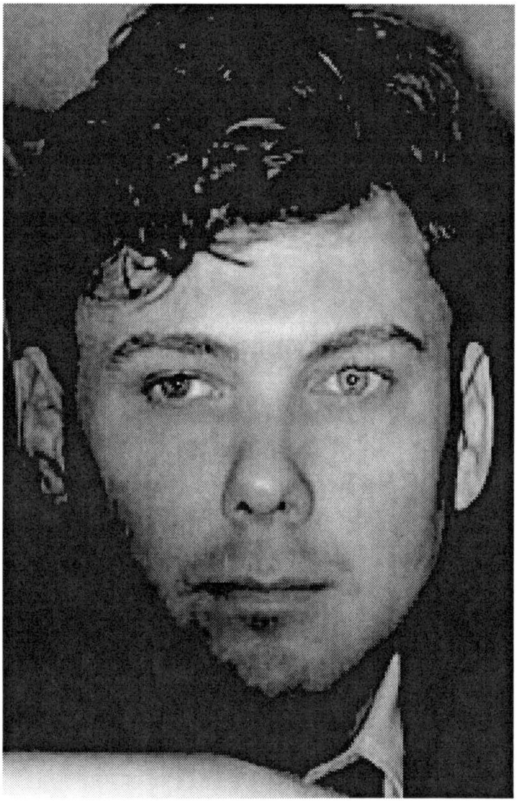

THE SCHOOLGIRL KILLER

Their crime spree started when Paul Bernardo discovered his bride-to-be, Karla Homolka, wasn't a virgin. By Paul's reckoning, she owed him a virgin – her younger sister Tammy. On December 23, 1990, after a holiday evening with the Homolka family -- while the rest of the clan slept upstairs -- Paul raped the drugged Tammy and ordered Karla to make sexual advances to her. They were videotaping the whole thing. Unfortunately, Tammy vomited and choked to death. Paul complained that he wasn't done and blamed Karla for spoiling his fun. Karla decided to find him a replacement – as a wedding gift.

Karla selected a fifteen-year-old who idolized her as a role model and bore a resemblance to the dead Tammy. Using the same routine that had killed her sister, Karla drugged the girl into unconsciousness and at Paul's orders performed sex with her. Paul then raped and sodomized their victim. Again, they videotaped the whole thing. When they were done, Karla cleaned the girl up and put her to bed. The next day she introduced her to Paul for the "first" time.

During the time that Paul and Karla were dating in 1987, he became the "Scarborough Rapist" terrorizing the Toronto suburb he called home. He grabbed women getting off area buses, raped and sodomized them. In two years he assaulted thirteen women. Karla knew what Paul was doing and encouraged him. According to the testimony of one of his victims, Karla may have gone along on the rapes with the video camera.

By the time Paul came to the attention of authorities through a composite sketch of the rapist, the attacks stopped. Even though Paul gave a DNA sample, testing in the case was not vigorously pursued and he was not arrested. This oversight allowed Paul and Karla to progress from rape to murder.

Paul supported himself smuggling cigarettes across the U.S,-Canada border, a business that also required him to steal license plates. In June 1991, while engaged in one of his nocturnal thieving sprees, he encountered Leslie Mahaffy, a fourteen-year-old who had gotten locked out of her home past her curfew. Paul kidnapped her at knife point, took her home, and went to work. When Karla woke up, she joined in. Two weeks later Mahaffy's body parts were found encased in five concrete blocks in shallow water in Lake Gibson.

Their next victim was Kristen French abducted from a church parking lot on April 16, 1992. They kept her for two days, degrading her in the most vile ways, until they killed her. As police investigated the deaths of French and Mahaffy they became aware of Bernardo and questioned him about the Scarborough rapes. He readily admitted to being a suspect. Amazingly, in February 1993 after all that time had passed, authorities got around to finishing the DNA testing, which proved Paul had committed at least three of the assaults back in 1987. Paul was put under surveillance. He was also facing assault charges – filed by Karla whom Paul had started beating in the summer of 1992.

When Paul was arrested for the rapes and the murders, Karla, who already had a good lawyer, began to paint herself as one of his victim's as well. In their home, police discovered Paul's written descriptions of each of his rapes. The couple owned an extensive video and print library of pornography and also had works on serial killers. Authorities discovered one video of Karla engaged in sexual acts with two women but the bulk of the video evidence had been removed. As Karla's complicity in Paul's criminal acts began to emerge, however, she cut a deal – two twelve year sentences to be served concurrently with eligibility for parole in three years, time to be served in a psychiatric hospital. All she had to do was testify against Paul.

When Paul came to trial two years later, the missing videotapes, which he'd turned over to his first attorney thinking the prosecution would never see them were the central and sordid pieces of evidence against him. In addition to the vivid and disgusting video evidence, Karla was called to the stand to elaborate on the images. When the defense had their turn, however, a portrait of the true Karla emerged. While Paul may not have treated her any better than his victims, she stayed with him willingly and was a woman without morals or conscience, displaying no real remorse for her role in their crimes. It also became clear she had manipulated the government beautifully to her advantage.

Paul was found guilty on all charges. He remains in prison. Karla was released in July 2005 under severe restrictions although they were lifted in November. Dubbed the Ken and Barbie of Mayhem and Murder for their picture-perfect good looks and apparent suburban lifestyle, both Paul and Karla are murderous sadists responsible for the torture and death of at least two young women. And Karla is alive and well – and on the loose – in Canada today.

JACK KEVORKIAN

Born
May 26, 1928

Also Known As
Dr. Jack Kevorkian

Number of victims:
130+

DR. JACK KEVORKIAN

On November 22, 1998 Dr. Jack Kevorkian allowed the news program 60 Minutes to air a videotape made in September of the same year showing the voluntary euthanasia of Thomas Youk who suffered from amyotrophic lateral sclerosis, ALS or Lou Gehrig's Disease. The fatal motor neuron disease causes the progressive weakening and atrophy of the body while patients maintain all their normal traits of intelligence, memory, and personality. Ultimately when the diaphragm and chest muscles fail, ALS patients require mechanical ventilation to breathe. Most individuals with ALS die of respiratory failure three to five years after they receive their diagnosis. Some ten percent live eight years or longer. It is, without question, a horrible disease, but does that make euthanasia morally acceptable? Was Jack Kevorkian a murderer for administering a lethal injection to Youk or was he a cold-blooded killer? The question is still one that is hotly debated.

Kevorkian was charged with second-degree homicide on March 26, 1999. It was not the doctor's first time in the court room. Through the years he had been tried numerous times for assisting in suicides, but this case was different. This time he and he alone had given the fatal shot because Youk was not physically capable of doing so. Kevorkian chose to represent himself, a serious mistake since presenting his arguments with supporting evidence proved difficult for him. Kevorkian was found guilty and sentenced to ten to 25 years in a Michigan prison where he is still serving out his time today. All his applications for parole have been denied.

Until recently Kevorkian indicated that he would, if given the opportunity, continue to assist terminally ill patients to commit suicide as an act of civil disobedience against laws he regards as archaic. By 2005, however, in an interview granted to MSNBC, Kevorkian changed his tune saying that if he were paroled he would campaign to have the laws changed but would no longer directly help people to die. The parole board was not impressed, however, and turned him down again on December 22, 2005.

During his career as a physician performing "death counseling," Kevorkian assisted in the suicides of more than a hundred terminally ill patients. In each of the cases the individuals themselves performed the final action that resulted in their deaths, pushing a button on a device constructed by Kevorkian that released the necessary drugs or chemicals to end their lives. In some instances this was accomplished through an IV, in others via a gas mask that fed off a canister of carbon monoxide. In the German journal Medicine and Law, Kevorkian proposed a system of planned deaths in suicide clinics. It isn't surprising that American journalists began to refer to him as "Dr. Death" while late night comedians performed routines of questionable taste with punch lines about "Calling Dr. Kevorkian."

With more than a hundred deaths to his name and his admitted construction of machines for the express purpose of causing death, Kevorkian certainly fits the numerical criteria of a serial killer, and yet many are reluctant to place that label on him. He did not abduct his "victims" and he did not seek to elude the authorities – if anything he sought to confront them. Ostensibly he did not plan to cause pain and suffering, he claimed to be relieving it. And yet, there is a grisly underside to Dr. Kevorkian's so-called good works.

He began his career as a pathologist, one noted for coming up with ideas that were odd at best. For instance he believed medical experimentation on anesthetized inmates including organ harvesting was acceptable. He performed photographic experiments on dying patients, taking pictures of their eyes in a supposed bid to develop a diagnostic tool to determine if comatose individuals were still alive. He advocated blood transfusions from the newly dead to the living, and then, tiring of these subjects, Kevorkian moved on to assisted suicide.

Perhaps the most horrific aspect of Kevorkian's career is the fact that he tainted a serious question of medical ethics with the air of a circus side-show. His obvious delight in the attention he received coupled with his publicity stunts to further his cause made it difficult to take Dr. Death as a thoughtful advocate for the right of the terminally ill to end their lives with dignity.

If Dr. Kevorkian is granted parole when he is once again eligible in 2007 he will emerge from prison an 81-year-old man. His is not a case of howling dogs inciting him to murder or of a homicidal maniac dismembering his victims. Kevorkian's victims came to him willingly, often in pain and desperation. If they could speak for themselves they might say the good doctor had done only what they asked him to do, but his very willingness to end the lives of more than a hundred people puts Kevorkian's motives up for scrutiny and earns him a place among America's most prolific agents of death.

CONCLUSION

In seeking to profile the careers of serial killers in the Americas, the greatest challenge is not in finding subjects but in narrowing them down. For as horrific as the crimes of the Boston Strangler, Ted Bundy, Henry Lee Lucas, Dennis Rader, David Berkowitz, Jeffrey Dahmer, Wayne Williams, Bernardo and Homolka, and Jack Kevorkian were, there are just as many more we could have mentioned – all with records equally chilling.

For a four-month period in 1977 and 1978, cousins Kenneth Bianchi and Angelo Buono worked together to rape, torture, and kill ten women ranging in age from 12 to 28 years of age. The press dubbed the unknown killer "The Hillside Strangler" because the girls' nude bodies were dumped at various spots in the hills around Los Angeles. Buono, who was convicted of nine murders, died in prison at age 67. Bianchi pleaded guilty to five of the murders and testified against Buono. He is serving his sentence in Washington state where he killed two women on his own.

In November 2001 police arrested Gary Leon Ridgway, the Green River Killer, for the murders of four women in the early 1980s. He later pleaded guilty to 48 counts of murder and has been linked to other killings, perhaps making him one of the most prolific serial killer in American history. Ridgway targeted prostitutes and runaways along Pacific Highway South and dumped their bodies in and around the Green River. Interestingly, two members of the Green River Task Force interviewed Ted Bundy in the hopes of developing a profile of the murderer they were hunting. When Ridgway was arrested, he had been a suspect in the case for almost twenty years.

Former pediatric nurse Genene Jones stood trial in January 1984 for the murder of two-year-old Chelsea Ann McClellan in Kerrville, Texas. Jones injected the infant with a drug that paralyzed her respiratory system. Prior to her employment in the small Hill Country town, Jones worked on a pediatric ICU unit in San Antonio where she reputedly injected infants and young children with Heparin to cause drug-induced hemophilia. Currently serving 159 years in prison, Jones' total death toll is not known but it is believed that from the beginning of her nursing career in 1977 she murdered fifty infants.

John Wayne Gacy raped and murdered 33 young

men and boys between 1972 and 1978, burying 29 of them in the crawl space under his own home. Gacy, who often attended neighborhood parties for children dressed as a clown, targeted young male prostitutes and runaways. His youngest victim was only nine, the oldest twenty. Unfortunately nine of his victims were so badly decomposed they were never identified. Gacy was convicted and sentenced to death in 1980. Because the lethal chemicals he received in 1994 mixed improperly, Gacy took 27 minutes to die, a fact that didn't bother the families of his victims.

In the 1960s and 1970s an unknown assailant called The Zodiac killed five victims in Benicia, Vallejo, Napa, and San Francisco, California. The case was officially closed in 2004 but no killer was ever identified although thousands of suspects were investigated. The Zodiac taunted law enforcement with a long series of letters including four cryptograms, three of which were never decoded. Chillingly the killer wore a black hood, like that of an executioner, with clip-on sunglasses over the eye-holes. A bib-like piece of fabric on his chest bore a white cross-circle symbol and he used a large-caliber handgun and a knife.

Richard Munoz Ramirez, the Night Stalker, committed a series of abductions, rapes, and murders in California in 1985. He was found guilty in September 1989 of thirteen counts of murder, five attempted murders, eleven sexual assaults, and fifteen burglaries. He broke into homes by night, immediately killing male residents with a single bullet. He kept women alive while he ransacked the residence, then he raped and degraded his captives repeatedly. Ramirez attempted to kill all his victims but some survived his vicious attacks.

In Tolmia, Colombia, Pedro Alonso Lopez was charged with 57 counts of murder, a number that rose to 110 as Lopez continued to offer up detailed confessions. It's possible that he killed more than 300, first raping his victims then strangling them, all the while staring into their dying eyes. He claimed he liked to position little girls bodies in grotesque parodies of tea parties. Lopez was quickly tried and sentenced to life in prison.

When 13-year-old Kim Ghelkins disappeared in 1975 authorities in Prospect, South Carolina decided to investigate the long-standing rumors that local eccentric Pee Wee Gaskins had his own personal graveyard behind his farmhouse. The bodies of three men and six women (including a two-year-old girl) were unearthed. Some were stabbed, others shot, and two died by drowning. Gaskins was actually executed of a jail house murder in 1991.Dr. Michael Swango killed one woman with an injection of potassium during his internship at Ohio State University Hospital and admitted to murdering three men in a VA hospital on Long Island. He received four consecutive life sentences, but did not answer for the entirety of his misdeeds, which probably run to more than 35 total murders between 1983 and 2000. An unknown number of Swango's killings took place during the time he worked for the Zimbabwe Association of Christian Hospitals in Zimbabwe, Africa.

They all killed in different ways and for different reasons. They practiced their own hideous rituals and established their own criteria for victim selection. All of these serial killers went unobserved for too long, blending in to the landscape and quietly taking the lives of the innocent and the unsuspecting. Part of their hideousness lies in how completely they did blend in. Ted Bundy said it himself when he described the role murder played in his life, "This activity is just a small, small portion of what was predominantly a normal existence."

OTHER AMERICAN SERIAL KILLERS

Charles Albright: AKA "The Eyeball Killer"; convicted of murdering three prostitutes in Dallas, Texas; sentenced to life imprisonment in 1991

Rodney James Alcala: AKA "the Dating Game Killer"; convicted rapist and serial killer.

Joe Ball: AKA "The Alligator Man"; killed at least 20 women in the early 20th century in Texas

Herb Baumeister: suspected of killing 20+ men along I-70; fled and committed suicide after remains of 11 were found on his Westfield, Indiana property

David Berkowitz: AKA "Son of Sam" and "The .44 Caliber Killer"; convicted of six murders in New York

Bloody Benders: family who killed guests at their inn in Labette County, Kansas in 1872

Robert Berdella: convicted of killing six men in 1988 in Kansas City, Missouri; sexually tortured and dismembered his victims

Kenneth Bianchi and Angelo Buono Jr: AKA the "Hillside Strangler"; killers of 13 women and possibly involved in three other killings

Richard Biegenwald: convicted of killing five people in the early 1980s in the Asbury Park, New Jersey area; suspected in at least six other murders

Arthur Gary Bishop: Utah man who murdered five young boys; executed in 1988

Lawrence Bittaker and Roy Norris: kidnapped, tortured, raped and murdered five girls in 1979

Terry Blair: Kansas City serial killer and rapist; active 1982–2004

William Bonin: AKA "The Freeway Killer"; with several accomplices, claimed the lives of 20 boys in California

Briley Brothers: three brothers and an accomplice responsible for 11 murders in the 1970s in Richmond, Virginia

Robert Charles Browne: convicted of two murders in Colorado; confessed to 48 murders

Jerry Brudos: AKA "The Lust Killer" and "Shoe Fetish Slayer"; killed at least five women in Oregon

Ted Bundy: law student who raped and murdered more than 35 women in six states; executed in Florida State Prison on January 24, 1989

David Carpenter: AKA the "Trailside Killer"; murdered five women on San Francisco-area hiking trails between 1979 and 1981

Michael Bear Carson and Suzan Carson: nomadic

hippie killers involved in the counter-culture movement; suspects in 12 homicides; sentenced to life imprisonment for three San Francisco Bay Area murders in 1983

Dean Carter: murdered at least four women

Richard Chase: AKA "The Vampire of Sacramento"; murdered six people in California the 1970s

Doug Clark and Carol M. Bundy: AKA "Sunset Strip Killers"; killed at least seven people during 1980

Carroll Cole: killed 16 people between 1948 and 1980; executed in 1985

Alton Coleman and Debra Denise Brown: multi-state killers whose killings took place during two months in 1984; convicted of murder in three states

Ray Copeland and Faye Copeland: oldest couple ever sentenced to death in the United States at the ages of 75 and 69; convicted of killing five men; modus operandi was to hire unskilled drifters as farm hands and later kill them

Dean Corll, Elmer Wayne Henley and David Brooks: committed the Houston Mass Murders in the 1970s

Juan Corona: California killer convicted of murdering 25 men in 1971

Andre Crawford a convicted serial killer, who killed 11 women between 1993 to 1997

Charles Cullen: nurse in New Jersey and Pennsylvania who killed as many as 40 patients through lethal injection

Jeffrey Dahmer: Milwaukee, Wisconsin cannibal who kept heads, skulls and body parts in his apartment for sexual gratification; convicted of 15 murders, but believed responsible for at least two others

Albert DeSalvo: AKA "The Boston Strangler"; convicted of unrelated rapes; DeSalvo was never indicted for the Strangler murders, although he did confess to them

Westley Allan Dodd: raped and murdered three boys in 1989; executed on January 5, 1993

Ronald Dominique: confessed to raping and murdering at least 23 men in Louisiana; sentenced to eight life sentences in 2008

Nannie Doss: AKA "The Giggling Granny" and "The Jolly Black Widow"; serial poisoner who killed 11 family members

Paul Durousseau: murdered seven in southeast United States between 1997 and 2003; may have killed while stationed in Germany with the Army

Mack Ray Edwards: convicted of murdering three children after confessing to the murders of six in Los Angeles County between 1953 and 1969; claimed at one point to have killed as many as 18

Raymond Fernandez and Martha Beck: AKA the "Lonely Hearts Killers"; killed at least three women and one child in the 1940s but suspected in up to 20 murders in New York and Michigan

Albert Fish: AKA the "Werewolf of Wisteria"; sadist and pedophile who cannibalized several children; convicted of one murder, confessed to 2 others,claimed to have molested 100 children

Wayne Adam Ford: AKA "Wayward Wayne"; confessed to murdering four women; believed to have killed others

Kendall Francois: serial killer from Poughkeepsie, New York who targeted prostitutes; after strangling the women, he would store them in various crawl spaces in and around his home

Joseph Paul Franklin: racist serial killer who targeted interracial couples and attempted to assassinate Larry Flynt and Vernon Jordan; convicted of 11 murders and confessed to nine others

John Wayne Gacy: AKA "Killer Clown"; killer of at least 33 men and boys; kept bodies buried under his

Chicago home

Gerald and Charlene Gallego: AKA the "Gallego Sex Slaves Killers"; kidnapped, raped and killed victims in the late 1970s; most of them were teenagers

Carlton Gary: convicted of the murders of seven elderly women in Georgia

Donald Henry "Peewee"" Gaskins: AKA "Meanest Man in America"; convicted of nine murders; confessed to more than 200; executed on September 6, 1991

Ed Gein: two known victims, one suspected victim, four missing persons; elements of Gein's life and crimes have inspired, at least in part, the films Psycho and The Texas Chain Saw Massacre, and the novel/movie The Silence of the Lambs

Janie Lou Gibbs: Georgia poisoner who killed five family members

Kristen Gilbert: AKA the "Angel of Death"; nurse convicted of killing four by epinephrine injection

Lorenzo Gilyard: killed up to 13 prostitutes in the Kansas City area 1977 to 1993

Harvey Glatman: Californian rapist and killer of three women; lured women to pose for "bondage photographs"; executed September 18, 1959

Jeffrey Gorton: convicted of two rape-murders in Michigan, suspected of more

Dana Sue Gray: convicted of murder of three elderly women and attempted murder of a fourth in California

Vaughn Greenwood: convicted of nine counts of murder, including eight of the "Skid Row Slasher" killings in southern California

Belle Gunness: Norwegian-born murder-for-profit killer who killed her suitors and children in Indiana

Anna Marie Hahn: German-born murder-for-profit killer who poisoned five elderly men; executed in 1938

Robert Hansen: Alaskan baker who killed prostitutes at his cabin; convicted of four murders but admitted to 11 others

Donald Harvey: AKA "Angel of Death"; hospital orderly; confessed to more than 80 "mercy killings" with 37 confirmed killings

William Heirens: AKA "The Lipstick Killer"; confessed to three murders spanning from June 1945 to January 1946

Dr. H. H. Holmes: active from 1890 to 1894 during Chicago's 1893 World's Columbian Exposition; convicted of only one murder but definitively tied to at least eight more and confessed to a total of 27

Waneta Hoyt: New York woman who murdered her five children

Michael Hughes: killed four women in the Los Angeles area between 1992 and 1993; charged in 2008 with raping and murdering four additional women between 1986 and 1993

Leslie Irvin: AKA "Mad Dog"; convicted of killing six people in Indiana in the mid-1950s; his Supreme Court case set a precedent for fair trials of highly publicized defendants

Phillip Carl Jablonski: killed at least four women in California and Utah

Keith Hunter Jesperson: Canadian serial killer convicted in the United States

Vincent Johnson: AKA the "Brooklyn Strangler"; a homeless crack addict who killed at least five prostitutes

Genene Jones: Texas pediatric nurse who poisoned infants in her care; convicted of only one murder but suspected of 10 or more others

Patrick Kearney: necrophiliac convicted of 21 murders in California and admitted to seven other murders

Edmund Kemper: started killing when he was 15 years old in Santa Cruz, California; convicted of six murders and implicated in four others

Tillie Klimek: Chicago woman who poisoned five husbands; sentenced to life imprisonment

Paul John Knowles: raped and murdered 18 people

Randy Kraft: convicted of the murders of 16 young men and boys; suspected of 51 others in California

Timothy Krajcir: confessed to killing more than nine women—five in Missouri and four others in Illinois and Pennsylvania

Peter Kudzinowski: killed children in New Jersey in the 1920s

Leonard Lake and Charles Ng: ex-Marines and survivalists; killed at least 11 people and suspected of 25 in Wilseyville, California; collected and murdered female sex slaves

Derrick Todd Lee: AKA the "Baton Rouge Serial Killer"; convicted of two murders; linked by DNA evidence to five others

Henry Lee Lucas: convicted of 11 murders and confessed to approximately 3,000 others, although most of his confessions are considered outlandish; a task force set up to investigate his claims suggested that the true number of his murders may be as high as 213

Rhonda Belle Martin: Alabama poisoner who murdered six family members; suspected of poisoning at least nine; executed in 1957

Michigan murders (John Norman Collins and Gary Leiterman): committed separately in Ypsilanti and Ann Arbor between 1967 and 1969

Frederick Mors: Austrian who killed 17 elderly patients by poisoning in New York

Herbert Mullin: schizophrenic in Santa Cruz, California who killed people to prevent earthquakes; convicted of 10 murders and confessed to three others

Earle Nelson: AKA "Gorilla Man"; necrophiliac convicted and hanged for one murder; implicated in about 20 others

Marie Noe: murdered eight of her children between 1949 and 1968

Gordon Stewart Northcott: AKA the "Wineville Chicken Coop Murders"; California man who confessed to kidnapping, raping and murdering nine young boys with the aid of his mother, Sarah Louise Northcott in the 1920s; suspected of the murder of nearly 30, executed in 1930

Carl Panzram: murderer, rapist and arsonist; convicted of two murders; confessed to 19 others; executed in 1930

Gerald Parker: AKA the "Bedroom Basher" raped and murdered five women and killed the unborn baby of a sixth woman in Orange County, California

Christopher Peterson: AKA the "Shotgun Killer", confessed to shooting seven people with a shotgun in a killing spree spanning from October 30, 1990 to December 18, 1990 in Indiana.

Dorothea Puente: convicted of three killings in Sacramento, California during the 1980s; suspected of six others

Dennis Rader: AKA the "BTK Killer"; killed ten people between 1974 and 1991 in Sedgwick County, Kansas

Richard Ramirez: AKA the "Night Stalker"; terrorized Los Angeles in 1984 and 1985; convicted of 14 murders

David Parker Ray: convicted of rape and torture and sentenced to 224 years in prison; FBI believes he was responsible for the deaths of 60 women in Truth or Consequences, New Mexico

Paul Dennis Reid: killed seven people during armed robberies between February and April 1997

Ángel Maturino Reséndiz: killed nine people in Texas, Kentucky, and Illinois

Gary Ridgway: AKA the "Green River Killer"; convicted of murdering 48 women in Washington state

Joel Rifkin: murdered 17 women in the New York City and Long Island areas

John Edward Robinson: AKA the "Cyber Sex Killer"; lured victims through the internet; convicted of murdering six women in Missouri and Kansas

Dayton Leroy Rogers: murdered at least six women in Oregon

Danny Rolling: pleaded guilty to murdering five students in Florida; executed in 2006

Michael Bruce Ross: raped and murdered seven women in Connecticut; executed May 13, 2005

Efren Saldivar: respiratory therapist who killed six patients, possibly as many as 120

Altemio Sanchez: AKA the "Bike Path Rapist"; responsible for three murders and numerous rapes spanning a 25-year period in Buffalo, New York;

currently serving three consecutive 75 years-to-life sentences for the murders

Heriberto Seda: New York City copycat killer of the "Zodiac Killer" active from 1990 to 1994; convicted of shooting eight individuals, killing three; sentenced to life imprisonment in 1998

Gerard John Schaefer: Florida police officer who killed up to 34 women and girls

Tommy Lynn Sells: convicted of only one murder; admitted to murdering dozens of people across the United States, possibly in excess of 70 although only six are confirmed

Serial Shooter (Dale S. Hausner and Samuel John Dieteman): Convicted of killing 8 people in random drive-by shootings in 2006 in Phoenix, Arizona

Arthur Shawcross: AKA "The Genesee River Killer"; convicted of 12 murders; confessed to one more

Robert Shulman: convicted of murdering five prostitutes between 1991 and 1996

Lemuel Smith: confessed to the murders of five people, including an on-duty female prison guard

Morris Solomon Jr.: handyman who killed six young women between 1986 and 1987 in Sacramento,

California

Gerald Stano: convicted murderer of 41 women; executed in 1998

Cary Stayner: killed four women in Yosemite, California

Michael Swango: physician and surgeon who poisoned over 30 of his patients and colleagues

William Suff: AKA the "Riverside Killer"; killed up to 19 women near Riverside, California

Marybeth Tinning: New York woman who smothered nine of her children to death

Ottis Toole: Henry Lee Lucas' accomplice; convicted of six murders in Florida; confessed to but never tried for Adam Walsh's murder

Maury Travis: St. Louis area torture killer of 12–17 prostitutes from 2000 to 2002

Chester Turner: murderer of women in Los Angeles, California; convicted of 12 murders and linked through DNA evidence to another

Henry Louis Wallace: Charlotte, North Carolina killer of at least nine young women from 1992 to 1994

Coral Eugene Watts: convicted of two murders; admitted to killing 80 people in Texas and Michigan;

possibly guilty of 100 murders

Nathaniel White: convicted of stabbing to death six women in the Hudson Valley, New York area from 1991 to 1992

Wayne Williams: convicted of two murders; police claim his arrest solved 23 in the string of 28 Atlanta Child Murders

Gwendolyn Graham and Cathy Wood: Michigan duo who murdered five elderly nursing home residents in their care and claimed to have killed another

Randall Woodfield: AKA the "The I-5 Killer" and "The I-5 Bandit"; convicted of four murders; believed responsible for 14 others

Aileen Wuornos: shot six men dead in Florida; executed in 2002

Robert Lee Yates: murdered at least 13 women in Spokane County, Washington

LaVergne, TN USA
23 September 2010
198214LV00004B/154/P

9 781906 512491